Greek Mythology

A Guide to Greek Gods, Mythology, and Folklore

Ross Romano

Table of Contents

Introduction 1

Chapter 1: Who Are the Greek Gods? 4

Chapter 2: The Demigods 23

Chapter 3: Heroes and Monsters of Greek Mythology 29

Chapter 4: Famous Stories from Greek Mythology 49

Conclusion 69

Introduction

Are you looking to learn everything there is to know about Greek mythology? Have you always wanted to know more about the Titans, the Olympians, demigods and goddesses, or fearsome Greek monsters that dominate the mythical canon? Then you're going to love this book! We've pulled together everything you could want to know about Greek mythology into one digestible book. From the origins of Greek mythology all the way through to the most popular stories, this book has it all.

Greek mythology can be identified as the body of myths that were initially shared by the ancient Greeks, in an era of folklore; the tales told at this time often revolve themselves around the origin and the very structure of our world, the adventures and tribulations of heroes, gods, and mythological beings, and are the initial focal point of a lot of ancient Greece's rituals and religious practices.

Today, modern historians look to these myths to hopefully give them a better understanding of the political and religious beliefs of the ancient Greeks and their civilization, in an attempt to better understand their time on Earth and the ideas behind these myths in general.

To date, Greek mythology has had an incredibly large hand in influencing contemporary arts, language, literature, and culture in the western world. It continues to be an integral aspect of western heritage. For centuries, poets and artists have taken inspiration from Greek mythology and found it to still have significance and relatable themes, even in our modern society. It's highly likely that you will be able to find significance and connection with Greek mythology, too.

In this book, we will look in more detail at who the Greek gods were. We will go into further detail on the original Greek gods, the Titans, as well as their battle for power with the Olympians. We will also discuss the Olympians in more detail in chapter one, focusing primarily on the twelve members of Mount Olympus.

Next, we will go onto discuss the concept of demigods and what constitutes a demigod. Once we have covered a basic understanding of what a demigod is, we will move on to look at five of the most well-known demigods in Greek mythology and look at what made them famous in a little detail. Some of these names will be familiar to those with a piece of basic knowledge on Greek mythology, but some may be entirely new for you!

Next, we will look at some of the most lauded heroes that are documented in Greek mythology. As you would expect, some of these heroes feature on our list of demigods, although some of the people listed here may surprise you or may be people that you have never heard of before.

We will then move on to highlight some of the most feared creatures and monsters in Greek mythology and briefly touch on their battles with heroes—and the outcomes of those battles.

Finally, we will finish the book by looking at some of the most famous stories in Greek mythology. By this point, the characters in these stories should mostly be clear to you from the previous chapters, allowing you to sit back, and take in all of the beautiful tales on offer.

Chapter 1: Who Are the Greek Gods?

In this chapter, I will take you through some of the main Greek gods. Many people are aware of some of the more famous Greek gods—such as Zeus—but what about the other eleven Olympians, and the Titans that preceded them?

I will run you through each of these groups, highlighting the most important Greek gods and touching on their backstories in more detail and depth.

The Titans

Let's start with the Titans. Titans are deities within Greek mythology that were thought to have been around before the Olympians, which I will touch on in more detail later in this chapter. The Titans were children of the first-ever deities, Gaea and Uranus, also known as Earth and Heaven.

The Titans were made up of Tethys, Theia, Oceanus, Hyperion, Phobe, Coeus, Rhea, Cronus, Crius, Themis, Iapetus, and Mnemosyne. Cronus was the leader of the Titans; this role was given to him once he was able to best his father Uranus and wrestle the throne from his tyrant clutches. In later years, Cronus discovered that there was a prophecy that his son would ultimately do the same to him as he did to Uranus, and he went out of his way to try and prevent that from happening.

Despite Cronus's attempts to stop it, the prophecy was realized. Zeus stole the throne, thus ending the Titan era and beginning the Olympian era after the great war between the two, known as the Titanomachy.

The Titans in More Detail

Now that you know the Titans' brief history, let's run through each of them in a little more detail.

Asteria

Asteria was the daughter of two other Titans, Phoebe and Coeus. She was also the sister of Leto, and the Titan Perses was her husband. She had a daughter named Hecate with Perses.

Asteria was the goddess of shooting stars and nocturnal oracles. She was pursued by Zeus but chose to escape his clutches instead. She did this by morphing into a quail and falling into the Aegean Sea. She changed into Ortygia, also known as the quail island, and is connected with Delos's island as well.

Astraeus

Son of fellow Titans Eurybia and Cruis, Astraeus was the god of the winds and the dusk. Goddess of the dawn, Eos, was his wife; together they had many children, including the five Astra

Planeta, or planets as they are more commonly known. They also birthed the four Anemoi.

Atlas

Atlas, one of the more famous Titans and son of Clymene and Iapetus, was the Titan rebellion leader who opposed Zeus. Because of this, when the Titans lost the Titanomachy, he was severely punished by being sent to hold up the sky for the rest of time.

This ties into how Atlas is often shown as a large man with a beard, often bent over, due to the weight of holding up the heavens.

Clymene

Clymene was known as the goddess of fame and infamy, and married fellow Titan, Iapetus. Between them, they had four sons: Epimetheus, Atlas, Menoetius, and Prometheus. Her father was Oceanus, and her mother was Tethys.

Coeus

Son of Uranus and Gaia, Coeus' name translates to mean "to the question." Due to this, it is often thought that Coeus was likely to have been a Titan that had a high intellect and a curious mind.

He was also known to be one of the four pillars that separated the Earth from the heavens. He represented the north's pillar, with the three other pillars being held by his three brothers, Crius, Japetus, and Hyperion.

These four brothers were instrumental in the overthrow of their father, Uranus. This is because as the four pillars, they were situated in each of the four corners of the Earth, which meant they were able to keep Uranus held in place while their other brother, Cronus, used a diamond sickle given to him by his mother, Gaea, to castrate him.

Crius

As mentioned above, Crius is another Titan, son of Gaea and Uranus. He went on to marry Eurybia, who was the daughter of Pontus and Gaea. They had three children together: Pallas, Perses, and Astraios.

Like his brother Coeus, Crius was one of the four pillars keeping the Earth and heavens separated. He was the representative of the south pillar. In the Titanomachy, Crius fought alongside his fellow Titans, but without having a specific role of note. Once the Titans had lost the battle, Crius and his brothers were sent down to Tartarus, the Underworld's lowest level.

Cronus

Cronus was the last son of Gaea and Uranus, the leaders of the first-ever generation of Titans. He played an essential role in leading the revolution against Uranus; however, once in power, he became just as tyrannical as his father, putting both cyclops and the Hecatoncheires in prison before eating all of his children save one. That child would be Zeus, who would eventually overthrow him and begin the Olympian era.

Cronus' five brothers were Oceanus, Coeus, Crius, Iapetus, and Hyperion, and his sisters were Mnemosyne, Theia, Tethys, Phoebe, Rhea, and Themis. He went on to marry his sister, Rhea, and they had six children together: Hestia, Hera, Hades, Poseidon, Demeter, and Zeus.

Dione

It is believed that Dione was the daughter of Tethys and Oceanus. Some say that she was Zeus' first wife, and that she gave birth to the goddess Aphrodite. She was worshipped beside Zeus at one of the earliest Oracles in Greece, situated at Dodona. This shrine in Dodona has a prophetess and priestess, called the Pleiades or "The Doves." The Dove is Aphrodite's sacred bird.

Eos

Daughter to Titans Theia and Hyperion, Eos was known as the goddess of the dawn. She had one brother, Helios, the god of the sun, and a sister called Selene, the moon's goddess. She was betrothed to Astraeus, who was the god of dusk. Between them, they birthed many children that stood for each thing that happened during the union of the dusk and the dawn, such as twilight.

Of those children, Anemoi was the god of the winds, Eosphorus was the god of the morning star, and Astra Planeta was the goddess of the planets. It is also believed that she was romantic with the god Ares, which angered Aphrodite so much so that she cursed her with sexual urges that could never be satisfied.

Because of this, Eos abducted a range of younger men such as Tithonus, Orion, and Cephalus.

Epimetheus

Epimetheus was the son of Clymene and Iapetus, and the brother of Atlas, Menoetius, and Prometheus. The name Epimetheus derives from the Greek term for "afterthought." In Greek, Prometheus also has another meaning: "forethought." This is one reason why Epimetheus often appeared the less smart of the two, with Prometheus being seen as more intelligent.

The brothers Epimetheus and Prometheus were instructed to provide all new animals with their characteristics. Epimetheus began by offering each animal a positive trait. However, as he lacked foresight, he could not predict that by the time it came to man, he had already given out all of the positive traits. Because of this, Prometheus decided to offer humanity fire and the civilizing arts.

Eurybia

The seas' Titan goddess was known as Eurybia, although she is only a smaller deity and never featured heavily in Greek mythology. Daughter of Gaea and Pontus, she was also married to fellow Titan, Crius.

Eurynome

Eurynome was the third wife of Zeus and was a Titan goddess. Her father was Oceanus, and her mother was Tethys. She had three daughters with Zeus: Aglaea, the goddess of splendor, Euphrosyne, the goddess of joy, and Thalian, the goddess of good cheer. They were also known as the three Charites.

Hyperion

Hyperion was a son of Gaia and Uranus, and he was the Titan who represented wisdom, watchfulness, and light. He was the father of the moon, the sun, and the dawn. In some of the earlier transcripts, the sun is referenced as Helios Hyperion. Yet, in transcripts since then, including Hesiod and Homer's texts, Hyperion and Helios are defined separately, and Helios is marked as the physical sun representation. Interestingly, there is no mention of Hyperion in the Titanomachy, despite his prominence as a Titan.

Hyperion betrothed Theia, of which brought them three offspring, Selene the moon, Helios the sun, and Eos the dawn. As we have already discussed, Hyperion was known as one of the four pillars keeping Heaven and Earth apart. Although it is not written, many believe him to be the pillar of the east, due to his daughter being dawn.

Iapetus

The final sibling of the four pillars, Iapetus, was also the son of Gaea and Uranus. He was also the father of Prometheus, Atlas, Menoetius, and Epimetheus. Some deemed Iapetus the god of craftsmanship. However, others saw him as the god of mortality. He represented the west pillar and played his part in helping hold Uranus in place for his brother Cronus to castrate him with the sickle.

It is thought that Iapetus' sons were also the ancestors of humans. Because of this, they brought with them some poor qualities that led to their demise, and these qualities were also passed down from them into humankind. Prometheus was deemed intelligent; however, he was seen to have passed scheming down to humanity. Epimetheus passed on stupidity, Atlas passed on an excessive daring nature, and Menoetius passed on violence and arrogance.

Lelantos

Lelantos' name means "something or someone that goes unobserved." This meant that he became the Titan of hunters' skill, stalking prey, air, and the unseen. He was the son of Coeus and Phoebe, and the brother of Asteria and Leto. He married Periboa, and Aura was his daughter.

Menoetius

Brother to Atlas, Epimetheus, and Prometheus, Menoetius' name derives from the Greek words for "might" and "doom." Because of this, he was seen as the Titan god of rash action and violent anger.

After losing the great war of the gods, Zeus killed Menoetius and sent him to Tartarus.

Metis

Daughter to Tethys and Oceanus, Metis was Zeus' first wife, and the goddess of prudence, deep thought, and wisdom. There was a prophecy that Metis would give birth to two offspring, one of which would be Athena, and the other would be a son that one day would overthrow Zeus. Zeus was scared of this prophecy, and so he managed to trick Metis into morphing into a fly, and then ate her. Metis was already pregnant with Athena at this time, and within Zeus' stomach, she created a helmet for Athena. Such was the pain that Zeus asked Hephaestus to take an ax to his head. Once it was opened, Athena emerged in armor and fully grown.

Mnemosyne

Known as the goddess of memory, Mnemosyne was the daughter of Gaea and Uranus. Also, going by Mneme, she slept with Zeus for nine days in a row, which resulted in the birth of the nine different muses. Within the theogony of Hesiod, kings and poets were in awe of Mnemosyne and each muse, which resulted in their excellent use of powerful words in great speeches.

Oceanus

Oceanus is one of the eldest Greek gods. Based on some accounts, he was born by the primal gods Gaea and Chaos, before being approved by Eros. Other accounts place him as one of the twelve main Titans, making him a son of Uranus and Gaea.

Oceanus was betrothed to Tethys, his sister, and together they had several children, known as the Oceanids. These Oceanids were lesser goddesses and gods that oversaw the sea, the springs, and the rivers. Oceanus and Tethys' high fertility led to floods, which resulted in them divorcing to prevent this from reoccurring. As neither of them took part in the Titanomachy and neither fought against Zeus, he allowed them to keep reigning over their water kingdom.

Ophion

Ophion was one of the older Titan gods in Greek mythology, and he was the ruler of Earth alongside his wife Eurynome, before he was overthrown by Rhea and Cronus.

Pallas

Son of Eurybia and Crius, Pallas had two brothers, Perses and Astraeus. He had several offspring with his wife Styx, named Kratos, Bia, Zelus, Nike, Scylla, Lacus, and Fontes. Pallas was the god of warcraft and was killed in the Titanomachy by the goddess Athena.

Perses

Another son of Eurybia and Crius, Perses was the god of peace and destruction. Married to Asteria, a Titan goddess, they birthed one daughter named Hecate, who became the goddess of magic, witchcraft, and wilderness.

Phoebe

Phoebe was betrothed to Coeus, and they went on to have Asteria and Leto. Her parents were Uranus and Gaea. She was also grandmother to Apollo and Artemis, two of the twelve Olympians. Because of this, they were often referred to as Phoebe and Phoebus, in memory of her.

As she did not fight in the Titanomachy, she was exempt from being imprisoned in Tartarus.

Prometheus

Despite being a Titan, Prometheus worked alongside his brother Epimetheus and teamed up with Zeus throughout the Titanomachy. Despite this, he began to argue with Zeus over Zeus' treatment of humans. Prometheus then proceeded to steal fire from the Greek gods and gave it to humanity. As punishment, Zeus chained Prometheus up and let eagles prey on him. After a long time, Zeus' son Heracles freed Prometheus by shooting the eagle, before Prometheus and Zeus reconciled.

Rhea

Rhea was the daughter of Titans Uranus and Gaea. She was the wife and sister of Cronus and was in charge of how things flowed within the kingdom Cronus oversaw.

Together they have six children: Hades, Hera, Poseidon, Hestia, Demeter, and Zeus. Cronus feared his sons might overthrow him as he did his father, so he chose to swallow each of them. However, Rhea saved Zeus, who went on to conquer Cronus and force him to disgorge his brothers and sisters.

Despite having a temple in Crete, which is where she hid Zeus from Cronus, she does not have a particularly large following. In art, she is often depicted as two lions pulling a celestial chariot. This symbol was frequently used at the gates of cities, such as in Mycenae.

Selene

Daughter to Hyperion and Theia, Selene was also the mother to Eos and Helios. She was in charge of pulling the moon across the sky every night and was therefore known as the goddess of the moon. She was also heavily linked to Hecate and Artemis, and the three were seen as the lunar goddesses.

Styx

Daughter to Tethys and Oceanus, Styx was one of the many Oceanid river sisters. She was the goddess to the river Styx, as well as being Pallas' wife. Together they had four children; Nike, Bia, Kratos, and Zelus.

In the Titanomachy, she fought beside Zeus and the Olympians.

The river Styx was known as the boundary line that divided the Earth and the Underworld. This was the very water that Achilles was submerged in as a child, which resulted in him becoming invincible. However, his mother held him by his heels as she dipped him, which meant that part of his body was still vulnerable. That is where the term "Achilles' heel" comes from.

Tethys

Married to Oceanus, Tethys was the daughter of Gaea and Uranus. She birthed the river gods who lived in these rivers and were known as the Oceanids. Even though she is the mother to so many different deities in Greek mythology, Tethys was not widely worshipped. As the Titanomachy was ongoing, Rhea brought Hera to her, and she raised her as her own.

Thea

Thea was another child of Gaea and Uranus, and her name means "divine" or "goddess." She was renowned for being a beautiful goddess, and as such, was the goddess of light. Thea was betrothed to Hyperion and birthed Selene, Helios, and Eos.

Themis

Finally, we come to Themis. Another daughter of Gaea and Uranus, Themis was the representation of moral order. She is also known as Zeus' second wife in a marriage, which allowed Zeus to reaffirm his control over both the gods and the humans.

Themis was also in charge of all undisputed order and law. She crafted the divine laws that all of the gods followed.

The Olympians

The Olympians were the Greek gods who went on to overthrow the Titans; they were made up mainly of third and fourth generations of the Titans, and because of this, they were worshipped as gods of the Greek pantheon. They were called the Olympians, as they lived on top of Mount Olympus. They managed to overcome the Titan ruling after a ten-year war in which Zeus led the charge, with his siblings helping him overcome the Titans and Zeus's own father.

The Olympians consisted of several first-generation Olympians, the children of some Titans, and Zeus' own offspring. Despite Hades being a significant and essential deity in the Greek pantheon and also being Zeus' brother, he rules over the

Underworld, a long way away from Olympus. Because of this, he is not considered to be one of the Olympians.

In this section of the book, we will focus mainly on the first twelve Olympians, although there are many that followed that many be deemed to be Olympians as well. Heracles, for example, resided at Olympus after his apotheosis before marrying another Olympian, Hebe.

The Twelve Gods

There is no confirmed list of the exact twelve Olympian gods. However, there are certain Greek gods and goddesses that are most often chosen to be seen as the twelve first Olympians.

Zeus

Zeus is probably the most universally known and commonly portrayed Greek god from any era. He was the ruler of Mount Olympus and king of the other Greek gods. He was the god of thunder, lightning, law, justice, order, and the sky.

He was the youngest child of Rhea and Cronus, the Titans, and the brother of Poseidon, Hades, Hestia, Demeter, and Hera, who he later married, despite having many lovers. His symbols included the eagle, an oak tree, a bull, a scepter, scales, and a thunderbolt.

Hera

Zeus' wife and queen of the gods, Hera was the goddess of women, childbirth, family, and marriage. She was the youngest daughter of the Titans Rhea and Cronus, making her the sister of Zeus.

As she was the goddess of marriage, she would often seek revenge on the lovers of Zeus and their offspring. Her symbols were the cow, the cuckoo, and the peacock.

Poseidon

Another very well-known Olympian, Poseidon was the Greek god of water, storms, the seas, earthquakes, hurricanes, and horses. Poseidon was the middle child of Rhea and Cronus, making him the brother of Hades and Zeus. He was married to the Nereid Amphitrite, goddess of the sea. However, like other Greek gods, he had a fair few different lovers. His symbols were the bull, horse, trident, and dolphin.

Demeter

Demeter was the Olympian goddess of fertility, harvest, nature, agriculture, and the four seasons. She looked over the fertility of the Earth and its grains. She was also a lover of both Zeus and Poseidon, and birthed Persephone. Her symbols included wheat, poppy, torch, the pig, and cornucopia.

Athena

Athena is the daughter of Zeus and the goddess of warfare, handicraft, and wisdom. She rose fully grown from her father's head and fought beside him in the Titanomachy. Her symbols are the olive tree and the owl.

Apollo

God of the sun, philosophy, light, prophecy, truth, poetry, archery, inspiration, arts, medicine, music, manly beauty, plague, and healing, Apollo is another essential Olympian. He is the twin brother of Artemis and the son of Leto and Zeus. His symbols include a mouse, a swan, a lyre, a bow and arrow, and the sun.

Artemis

Goddess of virginity, wilderness, and the hunt, Artemis is the daughter of Leto and Zeus, and Apollo is her twin brother. Her symbols include a horse, a deer, a hound, a snake, and the moon.

Ares

Ares was renowned as the god of violence, bloodshed, manly virtues, and war. He was a son of Hera and Zeus, and was hated by almost all the other gods, apart from Aphrodite. His symbols include the serpent, the dog, the spear, the shield, the boar, and the vulture.

Aphrodite

Known as the goddess of pleasure, love, passion, fertility, procreation, desire, and beauty, Aphrodite was Zeus' daughter and one of the Oceanids, known as Dione. There is also a theory that she was born via Uranus' blood falling into the sea once he was castrated at his son Cronus' hands. She was married to Hephaestus, but she had several affairs, including one with Ares. Her symbols are known to be the apple, dove, swan, bee, and the rose.

Hephaestus

The main craftsman and blacksmith to all of the gods, Hephaestus was, of course, known as the god of craftsmanship, forgery, invention, volcanos, and fire. He was married to Aphrodite. He is a son of Hera, and his symbols were the anvil, fire, a donkey, a hammer, an axe, some tongues, and a quail.

Hermes

Another extremely popular and well-known Greek god, Hermes was the messenger of the gods, as well as being the god of diplomacy, travel, communication, commerce, eloquence, games, and borders. He was even the guide for dead souls. He was another son of Zeus and is the second youngest Olympian, only behind Dionysus.

These eleven are the most commonly found as part of the twelve Olympians. The last Olympian is usually either Dionysus or Hestia, depending on the source.

Hestia

Hestia, goddess of fire, is one of the first-generation Olympians—so she is often deemed to be one of the original twelve Olympians.

She is the elder sister of Hera, Zeus, Hades, Poseidon, and Demeter. In recent times it has been speculated that she gave her throne to Dionysus to keep the peace.

Dionysus

Dionysus is the only Olympian to have a mortal mother, princess Semele. He is also a son of Zeus and the god of the grapevine, wine, festivity, madness, resurrection, and ecstasy.

Chapter 2: The Demigods

Now that we have discussed the main gods in Greek mythology, from the Titan era to the Olympians, it is time to look at the role that demigods play within Greek mythology.

In this chapter, we will discuss exactly what constitutes a demigod, before identifying some of the most powerful demigods documented with Greek mythology. This chapter will provide you with a better insight into the difference between gods and demigods, and will bring up a few names you may be familiar with (and some you may not be).

What is a Demigod?

The term Demigod is used in Greek mythology to depict a being that has one human parent and one godly parent. The godly parent does not have to be one of the main Olympian gods I have listed in chapter one; it could also be a lesser god, such as a nymph.

Demigods that were born this way were believed to have unique and unusual gifts that were well beyond the realms of the abilities of an ordinary mortal. Because of these powers, demigods were often considered heroes in many Greek myths, in a range of different ways.

The stories of the demigods have influenced many generations of society and real iconic figures in history. For example, Alexander the Great was adamant that he was a distant relative of Zeus, who, as we know, was the king of the Olympians. From when he was very young, he read Iliad, the poem written by Homer. He was so fascinated by Achilles's story; such was his fascination that he is said to have taken a copy of that poem with him wherever he went.

5 Demigods of Greek Mythology

When talking about the demigods and goddesses of Greek mythology, the first words that will come to mind for most people are supernatural, courage, war, and bravery.

We have all wished at one time or another that we had some form of superpower that we could call upon, even if it were of minor significance.

Here, I have taken a closer look at some of the most prominent and noteworthy demigods and goddesses from Greek mythology to help give you an idea of some of the skills and talents that these characters possessed.

Achilles

Also referred to as the "Trojan Hero," Achilles is one of the most famous demigods in Greek mythology. He was the son of the King of Myrmidons, Peleus, and Thetis, the sea nymph, and is renowned for being extremely brave, courageous, and an incredibly good fighter. There are countless myths and legends that are written about him, some of which will be covered in Chapter Four.

As I touched on in the previous chapter, one of the most famous stories regarding Achilles is that his mother Thetis bathed him in the River Styx. Her intentions were to make her son immortal. However, she did this by holding him by his heels and dipping him into the river. This meant that Achilles's entire body was accounted for, apart from his feet, which made his heel his weak spot. That is why in modern-day society, someone's weakness is often described as their "Achilles heel."

Perseus

Another famous demigod, Perseus, was the son of the king of the Olympians, Zeus, and a mortal woman called Danae. His stories are some of the most famous in Greek mythology. King Polydectes once sent him on a seemingly impossible quest, which was to behead Gorgon Medusa. The problem with this task is that anyone who looked directly into Medusa's eyes would be instantly turned to stone.

To try and help him achieve this feat, he was supported by many of the various Greek gods. For example, Hermes offered him a pair of winged sandals and a sharp, curved sword. Athena, the Greek goddess, offered Perseus a shield that could also operate as a mirror to avoid looking directly into the eyes of Medusa. Hades even delivered Perseus a helmet that would allow him to turn invisible when he was wearing it.

Needless to say, Perseus was able to slay Medusa and save Adrema from a wretched sea monster before going on to marry her. Perseus then took Medusa's head and gave it to the Greek goddess Athena.

Heracles

Also going by the name of Hercules (the Roman version of his name), Heracles was the son of a mortal female named Alcmena, and the king of Mount Olympus, Zeus. He was often depicted as a man who was heavily bearded and draped in a lion's hide, as well as carrying a bow or a wooden club as his weapon of choice.

Throughout history, Heracles has never been depicted as having a high level of patience, or even intelligence. It is written that he was often prone to having a high temper and acting out in an irrational manner. In one story, it is written that Heracles became so frustrated with how hot the sun was making him feel that he threatened to shoot the sun with his bow and arrow to cool himself down.

As I have mentioned, Zeus' wife Hera was never pleased with Zeus's lovers or the offspring they had together. In the instance of Heracles, she bided her time until Heracles had become an adult before she sought vengeance on him for her husband's infidelities. She then cast upon him temporary madness. This curse made Heracles murder his children. Once he had come around from the effects of the curse, he felt an overwhelming sense of grief and sadness. To make up for the crimes that he had committed, he was ordered to go and undertake twelve different labors. These labors included overcoming the Hydra, which was a humongous snake with several heads; hunting down the elusive Erymanthian boar; stealing Diomedes' mares; imprisoning the bull of Crete; pinching the apples of Hesperides; capturing and restraining the dog of the underworld, Cerberus; taking the cattle of Geryon; garnering Hippolyta's girdle; murdering the Stymphalian birds; killing the almost undefeatable Nemean lion; apprehending the golden hind; and cleaning the Augean stables in a single day.

Helen

Possibly the most famous demigoddess, Helen was well known for her beauty, and was the daughter of Leda and Zeus. It is written in Greek mythology that Zeus seduced Leda by visiting her and morphing into the body of a swan.

There is a famous poem that has been replicated in film format as well, that Helen was the main reason for the Trojan War occurring. This was because Helen betrothed Menelaus, who was the king of Sparta, and the youngest brother to Agamemnon. However, Paris, the prince of Troy, stole Helen from Sparta and took her back to Troy. This deceit resulted in the beginning of the Trojan War, which lasted almost a decade.

Theseus

Finally, we have Theseus, the only Demigod on this list that isn't a child of Zeus. Theseus was the son of Aethra, a mortal woman, and Poseidon, the Olympian god. Theseus is well known as the slayer of many high-profile villains, such as Sciron, Procrustes, and Sinis. However, the most significant achievement that is attributed to him was when he slayed the Minotaur, which was the property of King Minos of Crete, and was being housed in a labyrinth at Knossos. This Minotaur was a particularly aggressive and strong monster, as it was half bull and half man.

Theseus was also known to have been held captive by Hades until Heracles came to his rescue. He was eventually tricked and deceived before being killed by King Lycomede.

Chapter 3: Heroes and Monsters of Greek Mythology

Now it's time to move on to the main heroes and monsters in Greek mythology. By now, hopefully, you should recognize some of the names in this chapter; however, I will also readdress some of the vital information about each god so that you are keeping track!

In this chapter, we will look at the most important heroes in Greek mythology. We will also go into greater detail on some of the most dangerous and greatest monsters that are depicted in Greek mythology, touching on their heritage and what they are revered for.

Greek Heroes

Achilles

As you already know at this stage, Achilles was dipped in the River Styx by his mother, making him invincible everywhere apart from his heels as that is where she held him as she dipped him.

Achilles is known as one of the best Greek heroes as he was one of the great warriors of the Trojan war, fighting on the side of the

Greeks. However, by the end of the war, Paris, the Prince of the Trojans, killed Achilles by fatally injuring his heel.

This story is one of the most famous in Greek mythology and reaffirms the current use of the term "Achilles heel" in modern-day society.

Hercules

Next, we have another demigod that has already been touched on; Hercules is widely regarded as one of the bravest, most powerful, and most beloved Greek heroes. Despite not being the brightest demigod, Hercules went on to be a famous and noble warrior.

However, as we have already discussed, he was turned insane temporarily by Hera and went on to kill his family. He then had to complete the twelve labors outlined in the previous chapter, which seemed almost impossible. Since then, these labors have become the subject of many different dramatical pieces and art forms.

Hector

Hector was the eldest son of the King of Troy and elder brother to Paris. As his brother's romance with Helen brought war to their gates, Hector was tasked with leading the defense of Troy's city in the Trojan war.

Despite the Trojans ultimately losing the war, Hector was highly regarded for his nobility and courage throughout. In Homer's Iliad, it is said that the outcome of the war was mainly down to the influence of the gods. Towards the end of the war, Hector is forced to fight Achilles, the prolific Greek warrior, and demigod.

Initially, Hector is scared and chooses to run, doing three full laps of the entire city, before finally overcoming his fear and deciding to stand up and fight. As the fight goes on, Hector discovers that the Gods favor Achilles winning the battle. Despite this, knowing that he was soon to die, he still fought in a valiant and noble way.

Jason

Jason was widely known as the leader of the Argonauts. The Argonauts were a collection of 50 heroes that all sailed the seas, trying to find the Golden Fleece. Pelias, who was Jason's uncle, stole the kingdom that was rightfully Jason's. He told Jason that he could have his kingdom back, but only if Jason brought him the Golden Fleece. The Golden Fleece was made up of wool from a ram that was magical and had wings, which became the constellation known as Aries.

As their journey went on, Jason came across many dangers at sea, such as the Sirens and their deadly singing. The story ends with Jason and the Argonauts discovering the fleece, using the aid of a sorcerer Medea, who went on to become Jason's wife.

Odysseus

Odysseus was the reigning King of Ithaca, and he was instrumental in helping the Greeks overcome Troy in the Trojan war. When the war had ended, he made the ten-year journey home to return to Ithaca and back to his wife, Penelope. Throughout his journey, his cleverness and courage shone through as he fended off monsters such as Sirens, the Cyclops Polyphemus, and Charybdis and Scylla.

When he finally arrived back in Ithaca, he had been away for nearly 20 years. He had to start by proving his true identity to his wife Penelope, before once again going back to ruling his homeland. All of these adventures are documented in "the Odyssey" by Homer.

Perseus

Perseus is renowned as one of the heroes of Greek mythology, as he completed many dangerous tasks, was a talented warrior, and was able to think quickly on his feet. He was the son of Zeus and

Danae, and famously slayed the great monster, the Gorgon Medusa. As you know, looking Medusa directly in the eye would kill you and turn you to stone; however, Perseus used his quick thinking and used the mirror in the shield given to him to calculate when to strike.

Once he had beheaded the Medusa with his sword, he carried the head inside of his satchel. When saving the princess Andromeda from being devoured by a monster of the sea, he whipped out the head of Medusa, turning the monster into stone.

Prometheus

As we have covered already, Prometheus was a Titan Greek god. However, he could see that the Titans were going to fall to the Olympians, so he chose to align himself alongside Zeus instead.

However, things turned sour between Prometheus and Zeus when he gave humankind fire. Yet, Prometheus is still seen as a hero in Greek mythology, as the reason he gave humankind fire was that he felt that Zeus' treatment of humans was unfair and unjust, and he wanted to help them.

Aeneas

Aeneas is one of the biggest heroes in both Roman and Greek mythology. He battled alongside the Trojans in the Trojan War, and despite being on the losing side, he was in favor with the Gods Apollo, Aphrodite, and Poseidon. This meant that he was one of just a handful of men that were not killed by the Greeks during the war.

He was also the hero of Virgil's Aeneid, and founded the city of Rome. He did this after being spared in the Trojan war. After the war, he fled Troy and headed to Italy, where he and his descendants set about building Rome.

Orpheus

Orpheus was known for being an extremely good musician and was the son of Apollo and Calliope. With the music that came from his fingers on the lyre, he could tame wild animals and stop the flow of a river dead in its tracks. Orpheus was married to Eurydice, and when she died, he ventured down into the underworld to find her.

He used his talents with music to soften Hades' heart, and Hades allowed Orpheus to take Eurydice with him from the underworld and back to the living world. However, there was one condition. He was not allowed to look back at her until they left the underworld, and he was always to walk in front of her.

However, the temptation was too great and Orpheus, who was desperate to see the face of the woman that he loved, turned around. Sure enough, Eurydice then proceeded to vanish forever.

Theseus

Theseus was widely regarded as one of the top heroes in Greek mythology for his victories against many different evil monsters, including the Minotaur. As mentioned, this Minotaur lived within a labyrinth, which was situated on the island of Crete. Each year, the residents of Athens were made to deliver the Minotaur fourteen of their younger population, for him to eat alive as a sacrifice.

Theseus was not happy about this and, by using a roll of thread that was magical and given to him by Princess Ariadne, he was able to find his way into the labyrinth to kill the beast, and then back out again afterward. He later went on to become the King of Athens and a revered warrior.

The Monsters of Greek Mythology

Next, it is time for us to look at the monsters of Greek Mythology. Greek mythology would have very few heroes if there were no monsters for them to overcome. While some of the Greek mythology heroes are extremely well-known, many of the monsters in Greek mythology are often not covered in as much detail.

This section will look in greater detail at ten of the main monsters that feature in Greek mythology, and the stories that made them so dangerous.

The Sphinx

Made popular in the tales of "The Legend of Oedipus," the first monster we will cover is the Sphinx. The Sphinx was a creature that many said had the head of a female human, a lion body, and wings like an eagle. The Sphinx is known for confronting Oedipus on his travels down the route towards Thebes. She blocked Oedipus from going past her and posed a riddle for him to solve. The riddle is not referenced in early writings of this encounter, though more recent and popular variants of this tale state that the Sphinx offered this riddle to the young man:

"What is that which in the morning goeth upon four feet, upon two feet in the afternoon, and in the evening upon three?"

To the surprise of the Sphinx, Oedipus was able to answer the riddle correctly. It is man, as they crawl as a child on all four of their hands and legs. As they become an adult, they then walk on their two feet, and as they become elderly and frail, they walk with assistance from a cane or long stick.

Because Oedipus was able to solve the Sphinx's riddle, she then threw herself off an extremely high cliff. In other versions of the tale, the Sphinx instead eats herself, out of frustration and anger at Oedipus's smarts.

If Oedipus had been unable to give the right answer to the riddle, the Sphinx would have strangled him before eating him, which was the case for many of the travelers that had gone that way before him.

The Cyclops

Next, we move on to the Cyclops, the primordial giants that were made famous in "The Odyssey." They are said to be descendants from Gaia, the earth. They were renowned for their incredible strength and high levels of aggression, and only having one eye, located in the center of their forehead.

Many were scared of what the cyclops were capable of, so they were cast into Tartarus's deep pits, along with Uranus, their father. The Cyclops was imprisoned there throughout the Titanomachy, where Cronus defeated Uranus and became the universe's new leader. Once the Olympians came into power, Zeus chose to free the Cyclops from their pit. As a thank you to Zeus, the Cyclops then proceeded to craft thunderbolts for him.

Possibly the most well-known tale that involves a Cyclops is within book 9 of the Odyssey, which follows Odysseus and his woeful travels. In book 9, Odysseus and his group end up in a situation where they are stuck in a cave and are trapped by Polyphemus, one of the most feared Cyclops.

Each day that passes, he would eat one of the captives in his cave while blocking their escape in the process. However, Odysseus was thought to be extremely intelligent, and he put that intelligence to good use to become free again.

The travelers brought with them wine on their trip, and Odysseus offered this to Polyphemus. Quickly Polyphemus became drunk and started feeling joyful, asking Odysseus what his name was. Instead of giving the Cyclops his real name, Odysseus instead answered with "nobody."

Once Polyphemus dropped off to sleep because he was so drunk, Odysseus and his remaining crew stabbed the Cyclops in the eye, making him blind. Angrily, Polyphemus shouted out to the many other Cyclops in the area, exclaiming that "nobody" had blinded him.

The crew and Odysseus were able to get free from the beast's cave by strapping themselves to the underside of the many sheep that surrounded them. As he was now fully blind, Polyphemus stroked the back of each sheep that left the cave as they went off to graze. However, he could not see that his hostages were attached to their underbellies and were escaping.

The Chimera

Made famous in the legend of Bellerophon, the Chimera was known as an extremely aggressive monster, with the body of a lion, a lion's head at the front, and goat's head at the back, with a snake where a tail should be. The Chimera was especially lethal because it could also breathe fire.

There is a brief overview of the Chimera in a passage of the Iliad, and that is the earliest recorded mention of this creature. The Chimera was also said to have been a female, as it is known to have birthed the Sphinx, which we have already touched on, and the Nemean lion. The Chimera was widely feared by anyone who had heard of it and was known to have been an omen for shipwrecks and natural disasters, such as storms and tsunamis.

But the best-known story regarding the Chimera comes in the legend of Bellerophon. Born as a hero in Corinth, Bellerophon was ordered by the King of Lycia, Lobates, to kill the creature, to help make up for some of the sins he had committed in the past.

Bellerophon knew that he would not be able to achieve this feat without assistance, so he chose to sleep and pray in the temple of Athena. When he awoke, he was welcomed before him by the goddess Athena herself, offering him Pegasus's services, a mythical horse with the ability to fly.

Once Pegasus had been saddled, Bellerophon headed to Lycia, straight to Chimera's lair. He knew that Chimera was a formidable opponent that would be extremely difficult to overcome, so Bellerophon went about hatching a plan.

He decided the best way to defeat this beast would be to strap a large piece of lead to the tip of his spear. Sat on Pegasus' back, he went flying towards Chimera. As the creature began to open its mouth, ready to burn Bellerophon with its fire breath, he threw the leaded spear deep into Chimera's throat. As the fire reacted with the lead in Chimera's mouth, it melted, and ultimately this caused the monster to die of suffocation.

The Empusa

The Empusa is one of the lesser-known monsters on this list, with very little written about it in popular legends or traditional epics. With that being said, she had a scary appearance, as well as an appetite for human flesh and blood, which is what makes her one of the most fearsome monsters throughout Greek mythology.

When the Empusa is depicted in any stories, she is often shown as a gorgeous woman, who quickly shifts into a monster with sharp fangs, fiery hair, and even the wings of a bat. Empusa is said to have been a demigoddess, operating under the will of the goddess Hecate.

The Empusa was able to lure young male travelers if they were traveling on their own. After they had fallen soundly asleep, the monster would transform into her other form, before feasting on their skin and lapping up their blood. She features within Aristophanes's "The Frogs," in which she frightens the Greek god Dionysus as he makes his way down into the underworld.

The Hydra

Made popular in "The Legend of Heracles," the Hydra is the next monster on our list. A creature that was similar in shape to that of a serpent, with reptilian traits, the Hydra was a water creature with venom so deadly that one single breath from the Hydra would kill any man or woman in range.

On top of its deadly venom, the Hydra also had incredible regeneration powers, being able to regrow any limbs that became decapitated with remarkable speed. It was written that two more would appear each time its head was chopped off, making it extremely difficult to kill. The lair of the Hydra was locked in an ancient area of Peloponnese, known as the lake of Lerna. Here, there was an underwater cave that the Hydra would hide inside, which was known to be the pathway to the underworld.

The Hydra is renowned as the second monster Heracles comes across along his twelve labors. To make sure the venom does not kill him, Heracles chooses to cover his nose and mouth before trying to slay the beast. Heracles begins by attacking the Hydra using a sword, but quickly notices that for each head that he chops off, another two grow in its place. The battle seemed fruitless.

But instead of giving up, Heracles came up with the idea that would help him defeat the Hydra. Once he had been able to chop off one of the heads, he quickly used a torch to cauterize the wound. This tactic meant that the Hydra was then unable to reproduce any further heads from that stump, and over time, Heracles could chop off all of Hydra's different heads. This defeated the Hydra and helped him achieve his second task.

Charybdis and Scylla

Another couple of monsters made famous in "The Odyssey," Charybdis and Scylla are two creatures that lived on either side of a narrow strait. Over time they've become so synonymous with each other that you would struggle to discuss one without the other.

Although never specifically outlined, the Charybdis was referred to as a terrifying sea creature that lived beneath a rock situated at one side of the narrow strait. It was known to engulf often large volumes of water, which created tremendous whirlpools that were able to destroy even the largest ships.

On the other side of the narrow strait lives Scylla, who was believed to have had many different heads and lived off the skin of sailors who had accidentally drifted too near to the sea creature's lair. This narrow strait leads to the term "between Charybdis and Scylla," which means being caught between two treacherous decisions without having a clear solution.

The stories of the Scylla and Charybdis are written in "The Odyssey." Odysseus was made to travel through the narrow strait as part of his adventures and chose to travel nearer to Scylla, in an attempt to avoid the large whirlpool created by Charybdis. As he sails his ship past Scylla, six of his men are engulfed by the sea created and then eaten.

This attack also ruined his ship and left Odysseus stuck on a small raft, attempting the narrow strait again. On his send attempt, he sails to the other side of the strait, where the Charybdis is lurking. His raft becomes trapped in the large whirlpool, but he manages to grab hold of a fig tree with branches dangling over from the shore, before being able to rescue his raft and quickly sail off and out of harm's way.

Cerberus

Cerberus is one of the more well-known monsters in this list and is also featured in "The Legend of Heracles." He is the loyal and trusted guard dog to Hades, a gigantic hound with three different heads. He was entrusted with guarding the entrance to the underworld. It was believed the Cerberus only had a taste for the flesh of the living, which is why he was such a good guard of the door the underworld, as he would only allow spirits that were deceased to pass through, and devoured any living being that was foolish enough to come close to him.

The three heads were intended to symbolize the different forms of time: past, present, and future. They represent the three stages of aging: youth, adulthood, and old age in other depictions.

Cerberus was a well-known creature of mythology, but he is likely best known for being the twelfth and last labor that Heracles was tasked to perform. He had been tasked with presenting the Mycenaean King Eurystheus with Cerberus, by bringing him from the underworld, only being allowed to wrestle him without any weapons. Eurystheus was the person who had initially instructed Heracles to complete these labors to make up for the sins that he had committed in the past.

Heracles was able to tackle the guard dog before using his brute strength to launch the beast onto his back and pull him up and out of the underworld. Upon seeing Cerberus on Heracles's back, King Eurystheus was so petrified that he cowered behind a large vase and pleaded with Heracles to take him back to the underworld where he had come from.

The Minotaur

A monster we have already mentioned in this book, the Minotaur, was a combination of the head of a bull and a man's body. He is most well-known for eating anyone who ventured into his complex labyrinth that he called home. This labyrinth was known for being impossible to get out of and was crafted by Daedalus, a highly skilled inventor. The labyrinth was housed below the palace of Knossos, which is where Minos, the King of Crete, resided.

The tale of the Minotaur starts with King Minos losing his son, Androgeus, who was killed in Athens. There are many different variations of this story. Still, one particular variant explains that he was killed as the local people were jealous and envious of how many victories he had at the local Panathenaic Games, held in Athens. Because of his death, King Minos began a war with Athens, which he went on to win. As punishment for murdering his son, he forced the Athenians to provide him with seven young maidens and seven young men, sending them to Crete, where they were sent into the labyrinth and hunted down one by one by the Minotaur.

One hero of Athens, Theseus, offered himself as a volunteer to be sacrificed to the creature. Once he arrived, he was supported by Ariadne, who was the King's daughter. Before Theseus was locked inside the labyrinth, Ariadne took him out of his holding cell and showed him the ginormous maze's starting place. Theseus then worked his way through the labyrinth and found the Minotaur asleep in the maze's center.

He used surprise to his advantage and attacked the Minotaur, killing the monster quickly and easily. He then managed to escape along with the other trapped Athenians and the princess Ariadne, and make their way back to Athens.

Medusa

Quite possibly the most well-known and most popular monsters in Greek mythology, is Medusa. A monster that had the potential to transform a person into stone if they made the mistake of looking at her, Medusa is well-known to almost anyone who knows a thing or two about Greek mythology.

There are a couple of different accounts for the backstory of how Medusa came to be. In one account, it is said that Medusa was born to Ceto, an archaic marine deity. In this account of the story, Medusa was birthed with a disgusting face and a serpent's tail in place of her legs. However, in Ovid's Metamorphoses, Medusa was described as a stunning young maiden who morphed into a disgusting monster after being sexually assaulted by the sea god Poseidon, in the temple of Athena. Throughout the different accounts, one thing is always the same: her hair was made up of venomous, aggressive, and dangerous snakes.

In mythology, Medusa is slain by Perseus, who has been asked by his stepfather to collect Medusa's head. As we have already discussed, Perseus achieved this by using a shield containing a mirror, that was gifted to him by Athena. Using the reflection, Perseus judged when to attack and behead the monster without looking directly at her. Perseus then continued to use the power of Medusa's head as a weapon when he came across enemies on his path, before giving the head to Athena.

Typhon

Referred to as the "father of all monsters," last but certainly not least on this list is the monster, Typhon. He was brought to life from Gaia, the earth, and Tartarus, the deepest parts of hell. It is believed the Typhon was the toughest and scariest monster ever to roam the earth.

Typhon was humongous; it was written that when he stood fully upright, his head would be level with the stars in the sky. His lower body was made up of two viper tails, and instead of having fingers like you or I, he possessed dragon heads in their place on each hand. It was also written that he had wings so large that they completely blocked the light from the sun when he raised them to take flight. So much was Typhon's power and might that even the great Olympian gods were afraid of him.

Therefore, there was only one opponent that even stood a chance of defeating him, and that was Zeus, the King of the Olympians. While his fellow Olympians ran scared from Typhon, Zeus stood his ground against this ferocious creature. They fought a great battle, which was so ferocious it caused several tsunamis, earthquakes, and other natural disasters. The battle between Zeus and Typhon was so great that the Earth itself was close to splitting into two separate pieces.

Ultimately, Zeus would overpower the mighty Typhon, casting one hundred precisely shot thunderbolts into a vulnerable part of the creature's skull. As a result, Typhon was sent to Tartarus's deepest depths, where he was to be locked away for the rest of time. Despite these intentions, the monster was unable to be held in peace. While trapped deep in the underworld, he would, on occasion, become extremely angry. This fury would lead to volcanic eruptions and other natural disasters on the surface of the earth.

Chapter 4: Famous Stories from Greek Mythology

Clash of the Titans

If you were to read Theogony by Hesiod, then you would read that in the beginning, the only thing that existed was Chaos. Vast darkness covered anything and everything, until one day, the Earth grew from out of the Chaos along with the mountains, the sky, the sea, the stars, and the moon. The sky and Earth then combined and brought with it the Titans. The sky, also known as Uranus, was scared that one of these Titans would attempt to take the throne from him. To prevent this, he decided to lock each of them down in the deepest parts of the Earth.

However, one of the Titans, Cronus, was able to break free and defeat him, making him the new leader of the world. He then freed his Titan brothers and sisters before marrying Rhea, and together having three goddesses and two gods as children. These included Poseidon, Hestia, Hera, Hades, and Demeter.

However, Cronus had the same fears as his father did, and was sure that one of his children would try and dethrone him. With that in mind, he decided to swallow them whole. What he didn't know was that Rhea was anticipating another child. Scared that the same fate would meet this child, she hid away and birthed him on a mountain, hiding the child there, and calling him Zeus.

She swaddled a stone and gave it to Cronus, which he then ate, believing it to be the newborn baby. The mountain Nymphs looked after Zeus, and when he got older, Zeus searched out his father and conned him into drinking mustard and wine, which made him throw up everything within his stomach. All of the children came out fully grown, and this signaled the start of the great Titanomachy. Before Zeus and his fellow gods finally won, this battle between gods and Titans endured for ten years. They beat the Titans and dropped them into Tartarus, which is the furthest place from the Earth.

The gods then proceeded to fight against the giants to make sure that they ruled the Earth. This was referred to as the Gigantomachy, which was another war waged for many years, but like before, Zeus and his siblings were victorious.

The Three Sisters of Fate

Goddesses Clotho, Atropos, and Lachesis are known as the Moirae, and in Greek mythology, are the goddesses of fate.

These three siblings had the power to decide the fate of humans and the fate of the gods as well. Gods nor humans were powerful enough to influence or change these three goddesses' judgments or decisions. Clotho was the youngest of the three and was in charge of spinning the thread of life. She was the creator of life, and her thread was spun once someone had been born.

Lachesis, the middle sister, was in charge of weaving the thread that provided peoples fates as they traveled through life. Her name originates from the meaning "to obtain lots" in Greek, which makes sense because her role was to choose humans and gods' fates from a range of different possibilities. It was written that Lachesis used to measure the thread of life with her very own rod, which determined the nature and the length of that being's life.

Finally, the eldest sister of fate was Atropos. Atropos was in charge of cutting the thread of life, which is when someone ultimately passes away.

Prometheus and the Theft of Fire

A popular story from Greek mythology that has already been touched on in this book is Prometheus' tale and the Theft of Fire.

Zeus was in charge of offering each of the gods a gift. However, Zeus was not a fan of humans, and so opted not to give them anything. However, Prometheus did like humans and felt bad for them, as they suffered without any help from the gods. So, one night, he climbed up the side of Olympus and pinched the fire that was in Hephaestus' workshop. He placed the fire in a hollow reed and sent it down to the humans. This gift of fire allowed humans to be warmer and use the heat to craft better tools to live an improved life.

When Zeus heard about this, he was enraged, and decided to drag Prometheus to the top of the Caucasus, one of the very highest mountains. Here, he chained him against the cliff edge with tough, indestructible chains that Hephaestus had crafted for him.

Each day, Zeus sent an eagle to the mountain, which devoured Prometheus' liver, before it grew back again for the next day. This happened for thirty years, every day, until Heracles, the demigod son of Zeus, eventually released him from the mountain and his ongoing torture.

Pandora's Box

One of the most popular Greek mythology tales is that of Pandora's box. As you already know, Zeus hung Prometheus to a cliff after he provided humans with fire, but that is not all that he did.

He also requested that Hephaestus create the first-ever female human, out of water and soil. Each Olympian was instructed to provide her with a gift of some sort. Athena provided her with wisdom; beauty came from Aphrodite, Hermes offered her cunning, and so forth. This woman was named Pandora, which means "all gifts" in Greek.

Zeus also gave Pandora a box but told her that she could never open it, regardless of the circumstances, and sent her down to

Earth to the brother of Prometheus, Epimetheus. Prometheus had already told his brother that he shouldn't take gifts that Zeus offers him. But Epimetheus did accept Pandora. Despite her best intentions, Pandora could not resist opening the box, and in doing so, she let out all of the evil into the world, including war, death, hunger, hatred, and sickness.

The Abduction of Persephone by Hades

Daughter to Demeter and Zeus, Persephone was a beautiful child who only became more beautiful as she grew older. The first time Hades caught sight of her, he instantly fell for her and decided he would kidnap her. He waited until she was out in a field collecting flowers with some of her closest friends, the Ocean Nymphs. Persephone had a particularly carefree nature, which led to her drifting away from her friends, on the lookout for the largest and most beautiful flower she could find. But when she reached to grab it, the Earth collapsed around her, and Hades emerged, riding on his golden chariot. He grabbed her and took her down into the Underworld.

Demeter searched night and day to try and find her daughter, but to no avail. After some time, the Sun felt sorry for her and decided to inform her of what had taken place. Demeter immediately went to Zeus and asked that she be returned to her, or that she would never allow the crops and flowers to grow from the land again.

Zeus decided to send Hermes, the messenger of the gods, down to the Underworld and request that Hades let Persephone go. But before he let her go with Hermes, Hades tricked Persephone into tasting some pomegranate seeds, in the knowledge that anyone who eats food in the Underworld would never be able to leave the world of the dead. Persephone was then brought back to her mother, but Demeter became very angry when she was told of the pomegranate seeds. It was Zeus who then suggested they meet in the middle. For each seed Persephone ate, she would be required to live in the Underworld with Hades for one month.

From then on, Persephone spent six months of each year in the Underworld, and six months on Earth, with the Earth, blossoming on her return, and the crops wilting and dying when she had to leave.

The Name Giving of Athens

Originally, the first King of Attica, Cecrops, decided to name the city after himself, calling it Cecropia. Unfortunately for him, though, the Olympian gods noticed how beautiful this land area was and decided that they wanted to call this area after one of their own and become the patron to it. The frontrunners for having the land named after them were the god of the sea, Poseidon, and the goddess of wisdom, Athena. To select a winner, Zeus declared that both of these gods should offer a gift to the people of Cecropia, and it would then be up to them to determine which gift they preferred, and as a result, who the city would be named after.

On a particularly sunny day, the residents of Cecropia climbed to a high mound to see the gifts that the gods were going to present. Poseidon went first and offered the people a spring of water from the Earth by smashing a rock with his trident. Poseidon did this to show the people that he could provide them with water and that they would never experience droughts. But as he is the god of the sea, the water was salty, and so the people were less impressed that they might have otherwise been.

Then it was Athena's turn. She decided to hit the Earth with her spear and sprout a large and beautiful olive tree from it. The people preferred this gift because it offered them oil, firewood, and, most importantly, food. They selected Athena as their patroness and named the city "Athens", in her honor.

Theseus and the Minotaur

This is another famous tale involving the Minotaur, and one we have already briefly touched on in previous chapters. The story goes that Androgeus, the son of Minos, was deceitfully murdered when he was in Athens. In an act of revenge against the Athenians, Minos decided to order them to bring him a dozen of their younger people every seven years, which would then be eaten by the Minotaur. This creature was half bull and half monster and was truly terrifying.

The Athenians were tossed into a complex labyrinth, to wander cluelessly, until eventually the Minotaur would hunt them down and kill them. Theseus, the prince of Athens, was not happy with this arrangement and volunteered to be amongst the men offered to Minos. When he got to Crete, he was introduced to Ariadne, the king's daughter, and ended up falling helplessly in love.

Ariadne offered Theseus a spinner of thread to tie to the start point and then trace back to get out of the maze once he had killed the Minotaur. Theseus was successful in killing the Minotaur, before making his way back out of the maze, following the thread as planned.

He and Ariadne swiftly departed Crete via boat and made their way back to Athens. On the way, they stopped on Naxos island to celebrate their love further. On this island, Theseus had a dream about Dionysus, who said that Ariadne was his future wife and that he needed to leave without her. Ariadne stayed, and Theseus went home to Athens.

Daedalus and Icarus

The labyrinth that held the mighty Minotaur is said to have been crafted by the world-renowned engineer and inventor, Daedalus. Deep under King Minos' palace, the king commissioned

Daedalus and his heir, Icarus, to build the complex labyrinth containing the Minotaur. It is believed that Daedalus learned such skills from the Greek goddess, Athena.

However, once they had finished their work, instead of being paid for their creation, the king held them captive deep inside the center of the labyrinth. He did this to try and make sure that no one would ever discover how to complete the labyrinth, with the belief that if the creators were dead, no one would ever learn how to get out.

After scratching their heads, wondering how they were going to escape, Daedalus came up with an ingenious plan to get him and his son out of there. They collected a whole host of feathers from several birds, before sticking them to their skin with a wax, creating four humongous wings as a result. They used these wings to fly out of the labyrinth, and then far away from Crete.

He had warned his son not to fly too close to the Sun, as the wax would be melted by the heat, and the wings would fall off. However, after they had both gone past the island of Delos, Icarus forgot this and got too close to the Sun. As expected, the Sun melted the wax, and Icarus subsequently plummeted down to the Earth, drowning in the sea. In memory of his son, Daedalus named the place where he fell, "Icaria."

The Myth of King Aegeus

It is thought that before Theseus went to King Minos' palace to slay the Minotaur, his father Aegeus, the King of Athens, requested that he swapped the sails on his ship from black to white when he sailed home, as a sign that he was still alive and had been successful.

Aegeus then waited with patience in Sounio, in the hope that he would see his son's ship return with a white sail. Theseus was able to kill the Minotaur and get out of the labyrinth alive; however, he completely forgot to turn his sails from black to white.

Upon seeing the ship flying black sails, Aegeus was so distraught at the thought of his son being dead; he threw himself from the side of the cliff down into the sea. The sea was then named after Aegean in his memory, and Theseus went on to become the King of Athens.

Perseus and the Gorgon Medusa

One other extremely famous tale that we have already touched on in this book is the beheading of the dangerous and murderous Gorgon Medusa, via Perseus' blade. Son of Zeus and Danae, Perseus was a demigod who set out to kill Medusa.

As we have already mentioned, Medusa's hair was made up of venomous snakes, and anyone who looked directly into her eyes would instantly turn to stone. Using the tools given to him by the gods, Perseus was able to slay and behead the beast and complete his quest.

The Fateful Love of Orpheus and Eurydice

Orpheus was widely regarded as the best lyre player on the planet, according to Greek mythology. He was so good that it is said he was even able to charm the rivers and the rocks with his tunes. When Orpheus fell deeply infatuated with Eurydice, he opted to woo her with one of his songs. Unfortunately, their marriage was short-lived because Eurydice was attacked by a viper, which ultimately led to her demise.

So devastated was Orpheus that he decided to travel through to the Underworld in an attempt to persuade Hades to allow him to bring his wife back with him. Orpheus successfully passed Cerberus, the guard dog, to the gates of the Underworld, by lulling him into a slumber through his music. He then proceeded to play for Hades and his wife, at which point they granted permission for Eurydice to go back to Earth, as long as they stuck to one rule: she would walk behind Orpheus the entire way back, and he was not allowed to look back at any point.

As they got closer and closer towards the world, Orpheus became skeptical of Hades' condition and started to wonder whether it may have been a trick instead and that the gods were teasing him, and his wife was not actually following him at all.

As he could not hear her footsteps or speak to her, Orpheus grew impatient and chose to turn around and look behind him, just a couple of meters from the doorway to Earth. To his surprise, Eurydice stood there behind him; however, because he had looked back, her body morphed back into the Underworld's darkness and she returned to Hades for the rest of time.

The Tragic Hero Oedipus

The story goes that Laius, the King of Thebes, had been given an oracle from Delphi, which stated that his son would murder him before marrying his wife, Jacosta. So, when Jacosta did give birth to their baby boy, Laius decided to tie his son's ankles together and demanded that one of his servants take the baby deep into the mountains and leave it there to die.

Despite this demand, the servant felt sorry for the small baby and instead handed him over to a shepherd, who, in turn, took the child to the King of Corinth and his partner, who had not been able to birth any children of their own. Subsequently, the child was then named Oedipus, which is the Greek phrase used for "swollen feet."

As Oedipus grew into adulthood, he ventured to Delphi, the location of the oracle that had professed that he would marry his mother and murder his father. He met the oracle, and was so surprised by this oracle's words, that Oedipus chose not to return to Corinth to ensure that he didn't cross paths with either his father or his mother. On his way to Thebes, he came across a man and killed him. Without realizing, Oedipus's challenger was Laius, his father, thus completing the first aspect of the prophecy.

Upon arriving at Thebes, he heard the tale of the Sphinx and how it ate anyone who was unable to answer the riddle posed to them. It was also claimed that anyone who could solve it and kill the beast would be given Thebes's throne through marrying Jocasta. He killed the Sphinx and married his mother, and together they had four children. Oedipus thought nothing of it until an epidemic struck Thebes. Seeking advice from the Oracle of Delphi, the oracle explained that in order to counteract the epidemic, the murderer of Laius would need to be punished for the killing. Through researching who this could be, Oedipus realized the harrowing truth. Jocasta was so distraught at this news that she hung herself, and Oedipus grabbed two sharp pins from her clothes and stabbed his own eyes, blinding himself.

The 12 Labors of Heracles

Another popular tale that we have already touched on, Hercules, or "Heracles," is one of the most popular and famous heroes throughout Greek mythology. He is best-known for the twelve labors that he carried out. Heracles was the son of Alcmene and Zeus, making him a demigod. Hera, who was Zeus' wife, came after Hearcles and tried to kill him, as she did with all of the offspring of Zeus' affairs. She cast a spell on him that made him temporarily mad. In this temporary madness, Hercules murdered his entire family before coming to his senses.

Once he had established what he had done, he made his way to Delphi, to speak to Apollo and ask him if there was a way that he could atone for his sins.

The Oracle of Apollo, Pythia, ordered him to travel to Tiryns and work for his cousin, King Eurystheus, for twelve years. Eurystheus hated Hercules, so he sent him out to complete twelve labors that seemed to be impossible.

These twelve labors are laid out in chapter 2, but needless to say, he was able to achieve each and every one of them and free himself from having to serve his cousin, as he had successfully atoned for murdering his family.

The Myth of Apollo and Daphne

The daughter of a river god, Daphne was a Naiad Nymph, famous for being a gorgeous creature that one day caught the eye of the Olympian, Apollo. Despite this, Daphne had decided that she was never to be married or touched by any man in her lifetime. It is thought that Apollo had been teasing Eros, the god of love. In retribution, Eros shot a golden arrow that forced Apollo to fall in love with Daphne, and he hit Daphne with a lead arrow, which made her despise Apollo.

Now under the control of the arrow, Apollo could not stop chasing Daphne, yet she carried on rejecting him at every turn. Apollo even stated to her that he would love her for the rest of time. Daphne sought the help of Peneus, the river god, and asked him to help free her from the grip of Apollo.

To help, Peneus morphed her into a laurel tree. Apollo used his powers as a god to turn the laurel tree's leaves evergreen. He also made the tree sacred and always opted to wear a part of the tree on his person.

The One-Sided Love Story of Pan and Syrinx

As the god of fertility and patron to the huntsmen and shepherds, Pan looked over all rural jobs, was the leader of the Satyres, and chief of all rural divinities. It is also thought that his parents were the Greek god Hermes and a wood nymph, which is why he was born with horns coming out of his head, the beard of a goat, pointy ears, the feet and tail of a goat, and a nose that was crooked.

Because of his appearance, his mother ran away in disgust as soon as she saw him. Despite this, Hermes chose to look after his offspring by covering him in the skin of a hare and carrying him all the way to Olympus in his arms.

The unique form and jolly happy-go-lucky attitude of Pan caused great humor and adoration with the immortals, and he quickly became a favorite of theirs, most notably with Dionysus. In Greek, "pan" translates to mean "all." The gods called him this due to the pleasure and happiness that they were all receiving from him.

Pan had an ongoing obsession with the Nymphs; he was very much infatuated by them, and he used to dance and play music for them as well. Some of the nymphs loved him for this, but others had a strong hatred towards him and instead chose to run away from his gesturing. Syrinx was one nymph in particular that Pan had set his eye on. She was the spirit of the reed tree, and he was desperate to have her, at whatever cost that might be. He chased her and chased her, trying to win her over.

To get away from him, Syrinx hid in the river by morphing into a reed tree, but that didn't prevent Pan's advances for long. He went to the river and began pulling out every reed until he spotted her. He then pulled her out of the river and began blowing the reed to try and release Syrinx's spirit from within it. He noticed as he blew that the sounds he was making were beautiful, so he decided to wrap several reeds together to create a large flute to make music with.

Goddess Athena and Arachne

The basis of Greek mythology was founded on humans following the orders of the almighty gods. However, that wasn't necessarily always the case. It is written that there was a lady named Arachne, which is Greek for "spider," and she was said to be very beautiful. She was extremely talented at the art of loom, and she was able to weave in a beautiful manner. She even went as far as to claim that she was better at weaving than the goddess Athena herself, who was the patroness of the art of weaving.

Her confidence grew so much that she even offered to challenge Athena to a weaving contest. Athena chose to weave a depiction of her battle with Poseidon, which was fought over Athena's name.

However, Arachne chose to weave about the adventures of Zeus and other Olympian gods with various women. Athena was so taken aback by Arachne's audacity that she transformed her into a spider and forced her to hang from a web for the rest of her years.

The Myth of Narcissus and Echo

Echo had a curse set on her by Hera, which made her unable to speak correctly, and caused her to always repeat the last words that were spoken to her. One day, the wood Nymph, Echo, was walking over the mountains, when she came across a beautiful man that nobody was able to resist, known as Narcissus.

Almost instantaneously, Echo fell in love with Narcissus; however, she was unable to talk to him because of the curse bestowed upon her. Because of this, she opted to stalk him in the shadows, keeping hidden and waiting for the right time to announce herself. One day, Narcissus noticed her presence. After an awkward conversation back and forth, Narcissus beckoned her out of the shadows so that they could make love.

However, once Echo stepped out from the shadows, he exclaimed that he would choose to die rather than to lay with a wood nymph.

Heartbroken, Echo sought shelter in a cave and stopped eating or drinking. She became extremely thin due to the lack of food, and soon her body disappeared completely, and all that was left was her voice. The goddess of revenge, Nemesis, took pity on her and chose to punish Narcissus for his actions towards Echo. She put a spell on Narcissus, which made him fall madly in love with his reflection that he saw in a pond not far from Echo's cave.

He was so in love with his reflection, that Narcissus was unable to move and ended up dying of starvation.

The Myth of Hermaphroditus

Son of Aphrodite and Hermes, Hermaphroditus was raised in the Mount Phrygia caves by nymphs. He had the face of both his mother and father, exuding beauty and grace. At fifteen, he opted to leave the mountain, which had grown up on and decided to head to Asia Minor, in the hope of meeting new people. Along the way, in Caria woods, he took a break to recuperate and have a drink of water from the Salmacis spring. There, lived a nymph named Salmacis, who was so in awe of how beautiful the young man was that she attempted to seduce him before he rejected her advances. Once Hermaphroditus thought she had gone and that he was on his own, he jumped into the pool for a naked swim. However, Salmacis appeared from hiding behind a tree and also jumped in, wrapping herself around him and calling to the gods to unite them as one. They decided to agree to her wish and merged the two bodies into one, which resulted in a creature of two sexes.

Bellerophon and Pegasus

Another of the greatest heroes from Greek Mythology, Bellerophon, was regarded highly for slaying many different evil monsters. The most famous killing we have discussed in this book is when he slayed the evil creature, Chimera. It is thought that he was a son of Poseidon and Eurynome. In Greek mythology, Bellerophon is often accompanied by the winged horse, Pegasus. It is believed that Pegasus emerged from the blood of his mother, Medusa, when she was beheaded after being tricked by the Greek hero, Perseus. Other stories write that he was born from a mixture of his mother's blood and the foam of the sea. Regardless, Pegasus was born a horse with wings.

At the time that Pegasus was born, large lightning bolts shot through the sky, along with enormous thunder clouds. This is what provided him with his connection to the elements of the sky. The tale goes that one day, Bellerophon stumbled upon this fascinating creature drinking from a lake and opted to try and tame it. Without the golden bridle given to him by Athena, this would have been impossible.

After he and Pegasus were able to slay Chimera, Bellerophon became cocky and arrogant and felt entitled to head to Mount Olympus, where the gods resided. This action angered Zeus, who sent down a gadfly to stab Pegasus, which resulted in Bellerophon falling from the horse mid-flight.

Pegasus carried on towards Mount Olympus and ended up becoming a loyal servant to Zeus. It is written that Athena saved Bellerophon's life by softening his fall; however, he was crippled and lonely, and spent the rest of his life this way.

Conclusion

There you have it, everything you could want to know about Greek mythology, from the titans and gods through to the most popular stories and myths.

You should now have a better understanding of how just how much influence Greek mythology has had on our world today, whether it be through the naming of cities, such as Athens being named after the goddess Athena, or particular terms or phrases, such as "Echo," "Narcissistic," or "Achilles Heel." It's truly remarkable how much of modern society still relies on different aspects of the tales told in Greek mythology.

Most people with little understanding of Greek mythology believe that it started with Zeus and Mount Olympus. However, you are now aware of the Titans' role in Greek mythology, and how vital the Titanomachy war was for Greek mythology as we know it today. In order to truly understand Greek mythology, this knowledge is vital.

It is interesting also to note that many of the ideas posed in Greek mythology surrounding love, vengeance, and cleverness are still replicated in today's society. It is no wonder that Greek mythology is often reflected in the film and drama industry, with the stories' feelings still being just as relatable today as they were then.

To recap, we initially started by addressing the main Greek gods that Greek mythology revolves around. This included the Titans, such as Cronus and Rhea, and how they toppled their father to reign over the world.

We then addressed the conception of Zeus and the other gods and goddesses of Cronus, while also discussing the battle of Titanomachy in greater detail, including how Zeus was able to defeat his father and then the giants to sit atop Mount Olympus in charge of all living beings.

We then looked further afield into the area of Greek mythology that surrounds demigods. You will now be aware that a demigod is formed when just one of his or her two parents is a god or a goddess. We also went into greater detail on some of the most influential demigods throughout Greek mythology, including Heracles and Achilles, to name a couple.

We then moved away from just looking at gods and demigods and turned our attention to some of the heroes presented to us in Greek mythology. Some of these names you would expect, as their popularity expands beyond just those interested in Greek mythology, although there might have been a few entries you were unaware of due to their obscurity.

We also touched on the different monsters and creatures that needed to be overcome in Greek mythology, going into detail about what made them so evil and dangerous, as well as a little more information on how our heroes eventually defeated them.

Finally, we looked at some of the best and most well-known Greek mythology stories, giving you a taste for some of the excellent storytelling that made Greek mythology so prolific.

I hope you've enjoyed entering the world of Greek mythology, and now have a greater appreciation and understanding of the gods, goddesses, heroes, monsters, myths, and legends that have endured for thousands of years!

www.ingramcontent.com/pod-product-compliance
Lightning Source LLC
LaVergne TN
LVHW011740060526
838200LV00051B/3264